What Firefighters Need to Know

Diane Lindsey Reeves

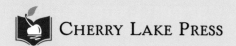

Published in the United States of America by Cherry Lake Publishing Group
Ann Arbor, Michigan
www.cherrylakepublishing.com

Reading Adviser: Beth Walker Gambro, MS, Ed., Reading Consultant, Yorkville, IL

Library of Congress Cataloging-in-Publication Data

Names: Reeves, Diane Lindsey, 1959- author.
Title: What firefighters need to know / written by Diane Lindsey Reeves.
Description: Ann Arbor, Michigan : Cherry Lake Publishing, [2024] | Series: Career expert files | Includes bibliographical
    references and index. | Audience: Grades 4-6 | Summary: "Firefighters need to have the expert knowledge, skills,
    and tools to put out the world's fires. The Career Expert Files series covers professionals who are experts in their
    fields. These career experts know things we never thought they'd need to know, but we're glad they do"
    — Provided by publisher.
Identifiers: LCCN 2023035060 | ISBN 9781668939147 (paperback) | ISBN 9781668938102 (hardcover) |
    ISBN 9781668940488 (ebook) | ISBN 9781668941836 (pdf)
Subjects: LCSH: Fire extinction—Vocational guidance—Juvenile literature. | Fire fighters—Juvenile literature.
Classification: LCC TH9119 .R4433 2024 | DDC 628.9/25023—dc23/eng/20230729
LC record available at https://lccn.loc.gov/2023035060

Cherry Lake Publishing Group would like to acknowledge the work of the Partnership for 21st Century Learning,
a Network of Battelle for Kids. Please visit Battelle for Kids online for more information.

Printed in the United States of America

Note from publisher: Websites change regularly, and their future contents are outside of our control.
Supervise children when conducting any recommended online searches for extended learning opportunities.

Diane Lindsey Reeves likes to write books that help students figure out what they want
to be when they grow up. She mostly lives in Washington, D.C., but spends as much time
as she can in North Carolina and South Carolina with her grandkids.

CONTENTS

In the Know

Every career you can imagine has one thing in common. Each one takes an expert. Career experts need to know more about how to do a specific job than other people do. That's how everyone from plumbers to rocket scientists get their jobs done.

Sometimes it takes years of college study to learn what they need to know. Other times, people learn by working alongside someone who is already a career expert. No matter how they learn, it takes a career expert to do any job well.

Take firefighters, for instance. If your house was on fire, you wouldn't want just anyone trying to put it out. You'd want someone who knows how to fight fires. You'd want someone who knows how to use firefighting equipment. If your pet was trapped inside the house, you'd certainly want someone who knows how to rescue it.

Do you want to be a firefighter someday? Here are some things you need to know.

Count On It

Math helps firefighters think like firefighters. Addition, subtraction, multiplication, and division all count. They help firefighters make quick decisions about fire hoses, water flow, and more. Algebra and geometry help firefighters develop critical thinking and problem-solving skills.

CHAPTER 1

Firefighters Know... How Fires Start

Firefighters know it doesn't take much to start a fire. All it takes is a spark.

This spark could come from a match. It could come from grease in an oven. It could come from an electrical short. Some fires are sparked by lightning. Sometimes fires are caused by intense solar heat.

Once a fire is sparked, it needs something to burn. Fuel for home fires includes paper, wood, and other household goods. Grasses, shrubs, trees, dead leaves, and pine needles feed forest fires. Igniting certain **combustible** chemicals causes fires and even explosions.

Parents take extra precautions to ensure that kitchen appliances cannot be left on by curious kids and cause a fire.

Some kinds of fire cannot be put out with water. In fact, adding water to them might make the fire bigger! These are called grease fires.

No matter the cause, all fires need one more ingredient. They need oxygen. It's a process called **oxidation**. This chemical reaction occurs when burning fuel mixes with air. It creates the heat, smoke, and embers of a fire.

TRUE OR FALSE?

Mrs. O'Leary's cow started the Great Chicago Fire in 1871. Or did it? For more than a century, her poor cow has been blamed. People said it kicked over a lantern. This burned down her barn. Windy and dry weather caused the fire to rage. It moved throughout much of the city. Ask a trusted adult to help you find information about this legend online.

If fires have fuel and oxygen, they will keep burning. It takes a fight to put them out.

Fires start from human mistakes, mechanical problems, or nature itself.

YOUR TURN

What three things does a fire need to burn?

CHAPTER 2

Firefighters Know... How to Stop Fires

Fires are easy to start. But they're hard to stop. Houses can catch fire and go up in flames in minutes.

A way firefighters fight fires is to cool them down. They use powerful fire hoses to blast fires with water. The water cools down the heat. They help get fires under control.

Firefighters use two other methods to fight fires. They starve it or smother it.

Starving a fire means cutting off its fuel supply. It sounds simple enough. You just remove the fuel source. This source may be household goods, trees, or chemicals.

Keeping a fire extinguisher handy is a good idea to help contain a fire if one starts nearby.

One way firefighters stop fires is through building trenches. They build trenches between a fire and its source of fuel. This is a common way to fight forest fires. Firefighters dig fire lines around a fire. These trenches are between 6 inches (15.2 centimeters) and 3 feet (.9 meters) wide. These breaks cause a fire to burn out. They allow firefighters to contain the fire.

Smothering is another method to put out a fire. Blowing out a candle is a simple example of this. Smothering is behind the "**stop, drop, and roll**" advice children learn. This process cuts off the oxygen supply and smothers the fire. With certain types of fires, firefighters spray foam to smother flames.

DID YOU KNOW?

Benjamin Franklin was not only a United States Founding Father. He is also considered the "father of our fire service." In 1736, he founded the Union Fire Company. This was in Philadelphia, Pennsylvania. This was the first U.S. volunteer fire company. Go online with an adult to find out more.

Three Ways to Stop a Fire: **1.** Cool it, **2.** Starve it, **3.** Smother it.
Spraying a fire with water cools it (unless it's a grease fire!).

But no two fires are exactly alike. If firefighters use the wrong methods, they could make fires worse. Firefighters must be experts in all the ways to stop fires.

GUESS WHERE MOST HOME FIRES START

Clue: It's a room where a lot of hot stuff happens.

Answer: Almost half of home fires start in the kitchen.

CHAPTER 3

Firefighters Know... How to Use Firefighting Tools

Firefighting is a big and often dangerous job. Special tools help firefighters do their job safely.

It starts with the clothes. Firefighters wear personal protective equipment called turnout gear. This gear includes fire-resistant pants. It includes fire-resistant coats, hoods, boots, helmets, and gloves. These items are not fireproof. But they protect firefighters from extremely high temperatures. Firefighters also wear an air pack and mask. This protects them from smoke inhalation.

Firefighters keep special tools in their turnout coat pockets. They carry rope, hooks, wire cutters, doorstops, wrenches, and flashlights. Seconds count when fighting fires. This way, they are prepared for any challenges they face.

Firefighter gear weighs around 45 pounds (20.4 kilograms)! Firefighters practice

Modern fire trucks have been around since the early 1900s.

Fire trucks are another important tool. For instance, fire engines carry firefighters, hoses, ladders, and water. They also carry other essential equipment to the fire.

Ladder trucks carry ground ladders and **hydraulic ladders**. Hydraulic ladders reach great heights. These help firefighters rescue people from upper floors of buildings. Firefighters also use them to direct water

Rescue trucks carry all kinds of equipment. This equipment includes things like circular saws. It includes cutting torches, cranes, winches, and **jaws of life**.

One of a firefighter's most important tools is physical strength. It takes muscle power to handle heavy fire hoses. It also takes **stamina**. Firefighters need what seem like superpowers. They sometimes need to break through doors, walls, or roofs. It takes a physically fit person to rescue people. People could be trapped or injured. Imagine the strength needed to carry an unconscious adult to safety!

NO TIME TO WASTE

When a fire alarm rings, firefighters spring into action. They must get dressed and on the truck in 2 minutes or less. Fires spread quickly. Firefighters don't have time to waste. There's no time to look for missing socks or boots. Everything must be in its place!

Your Turn

If you were a firefighter, could you get dressed in time? Grab a pile of winter clothes—coat, leggings, hat, boots, and gloves. Set a timer. See how long it takes to put the clothes on. Can you do it in 2 minutes or less? Practice makes perfect! The less time you take, the more time you have to save lives.

CHAPTER 4

Firefighters Know... How to Handle Dangerous Situations

Firefighters are famous for running into dangerous situations. They run in while everyone else runs out. Every fire brings the risk of injury or even death.

Even so, fighting fires is not what firefighters do most. Most fire stations get more calls for medical emergencies. That's why many firefighters have special training as emergency medical technicians (EMTs). These skills prepare them to provide **cardiopulmonary resuscitation** (CPR). They provide stabilizing basic and life-saving care. Then patients can be transported to a hospital.

Firefighters are also called to respond to traffic accidents. They may be called to respond to other types of emergencies. This is where they often encounter traumatic injuries. These injuries require urgent expert

Firefighters may have to help during traffic accidents when drivers face life-threating emergencies!

NOT THE TYPICAL SCHEDULE

Most people work 8-hour shifts, 5 days a week. Firefighters tend to work 24-hour shifts. They do this in a pattern of 1 day on and 2 days off. When on duty, firefighters live at the fire station. They fill the days responding to emergencies. They spend time training, maintaining equipment, eating, and sleeping.

TRUE OR FALSE?

Firefighters race to the rescue when a cat gets stuck in a tree.

Answer: Usually false. Firefighters need to stay ready to respond to human emergencies. They tend to refer pet owners to others. These other resources include tree and crane services. These services are better equipped for this type of situation.

SMOKE OR FLAMES?

Are flames or smoke more deadly during a house fire?

People are more likely to die from smoke inhalation than flames in a fire. Smoke in a house fire is more **toxic**. This is because of gases released from burning objects. Smoke puts carbon monoxide into the lungs. It keeps oxygen out. People and pets can pass out within minutes from smoke inhalation. They can even die. More firefighters are injured by smoke inhalation than by flames. That's why firefighters carry air tanks and wear masks. They follow safety rules to keep safe.

Firefighters know how to navigate burning buildings in the safest ways possible.

attention. This care is often provided in risky settings. These settings include places like the side of a busy highway. This adds to the danger.

Firefighters are first responders to fires involving buildings. They're first responders to forest fires. They also respond to all kinds of emergencies. Danger is just part of a day's work.

CHAPTER 5

Firefighters Know... How to Prevent Fires

Firefighters like one thing even more than putting out fires. Preventing fires is a firefighter's favorite thing to do. That's why they devote so much time to education. They educate the public about how to prevent fires.

Fire education starts with young children. Firefighters teach fire prevention lessons in schools. They host preschool classes at the fire station. They show off their big trucks in parades and festivals. It's all to remind children and families to stay safe.

Firefighters want all people to become fire safety experts. Some of the things they want people to know are:

- Smoke alarms save lives. Ask your parents if your house has them. Make sure they are working. Batteries must be replaced from time to time.

Sometimes firefighters visit schools to teach students about fire safety.
Through these visits, students can also learn more about what firefighters do.

Be extra careful in the kitchen. Forgetting pots on the stove is how kitchen fires start. Kids should never cook without careful adult supervision. Families should keep a fire extinguisher in the kitchen. Your fire department can show your family how to use it.

- Teach your younger brothers and sisters to never play with fire. This includes never playing with matches or lighters. You'll want to set a good example.

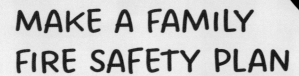

MAKE A FAMILY FIRE SAFETY PLAN

- Walk through each room in your house together. Identify at least two ways to escape from each room.
- Pick a place to meet outdoors so your family knows if everyone got out safely.
- Check to make sure that smoke detectors are working correctly.

Have family fire drills to make sure everyone knows what to do in case of fire.

FIRE! Every 24 seconds, a fire department somewhere in the United States responds to a fire.

- **Smoking is a leading cause of fire-related deaths. Does someone in your family smoke? Remind them to never smoke in bed. Even better, they should smoke outside of the house.**

Ask your parents to check your electrical wiring. They can make sure that cords are not frayed. Be sure not to overload power strips.

The first thing you need to do in a fire is get out. Then stay out and call for help!

CHAPTER 6

Firefighters Know... How to Find the Job They Want

Firefighters start their careers in a couple of different ways. They can start as volunteer firefighters. They can also start after graduating from a fire academy. Most go through a probationary, or trial, period. During this time, they prove they can do the job. It takes experience and more training for other firefighting jobs.

Types of firefighting jobs include the following:

- Airport rescue firefighters are specially trained to respond to aircraft fires. They work at airports.

- **Arson** investigators look into the causes of a fire. They figure out if the fire was set on purpose.

Engineers may drive the trucks, but every member of the response team is important when it comes to fighting a fire.

- Engineers are firefighters trained to drive fire trucks and engines. They are responsible for providing water. They raise ladders and set up hoses at fire locations.

- Fire captains are experienced firefighters. They have passed a special test to be promoted. Captains oversee a fire station. They're in charge of the station's firefighters.

- Fire chiefs are experienced fire captains who have been promoted. They are in charge of more than one fire station.

- Fire marshals are high-level fire chiefs. They specialize in fire prevention. They help identify situations that pose fire dangers. They make sure the problems are fixed.

- Hazardous materials (HAZMAT) responders are skilled in dealing with explosives. They know how to deal with gases and flammable materials.

WHAT DO YOU LEARN IN A FIRE ACADEMY?

Fire academies are where most firefighters get their start. Go online with an adult to find out more about what this training is like.

Fighting wildfire can be a dangerous job because wildfire can spread quickly and unpredictably.

- Heavy rescue technicians are specially trained. They rescue people in unusually dangerous or difficult situations.

- Hotshot firefighters or hotshots are elite firefighters. They are trained to fight wildland fires. They respond to emergencies nationwide.

- Inspectors are firefighting experts who inspect buildings. They make sure they meet fire safety regulations.

- Smokejumpers are skydiving firefighters. They parachute into remote areas like forests to fight fires.

Activity

Stop, Think, and Write

Firefighters are famous for running into dangerous situations when everyone else is running out. Can you imagine a world without them?

Get a separate sheet of paper. On one side, answer these questions:

- *How do firefighters make the world a better place?*
- *Is being a firefighter something you'd like to do someday?*

On the other side of the paper:

- *Draw a picture of you saving the day as a firefighter.*

Things to Do If You Want to Be a Firefighter

Lots of people want to become firefighters. Only the very best candidates get chosen to do the job. The good news is that you don't have to wait to grow up to start preparing for this career. Make sure you are ready to compete with the best of them! Here are some things you can do if you hope to be a firefighter someday:

NOW

- Do your best in school and be a leader for others.
- Find ways to get involved in your community.
- Ask your parents to arrange a visit to your local fire station. Ask the firefighters what it's like to do their jobs.

LATER

- Graduate from high school.
- Graduate from a fire academy through a local fire department.
- There are also 2-year and 4-year college programs in fire science. They are not required by all fire departments.

Learn More

Books

McCarthy, Meghan. *Firefighters Handbook.* New York, NY: Simon & Schuster, 2019.

Mobley, Paul, and Joellen Kelly. *American Firefighter.* New York, NY: Rizzoli, 2017.

Thiessen, Mark. *Extreme Wildfire: Smoke Jumpers, High-Tech Gear, Survival Tactics, and the Extraordinary Science of Fire.* Washington, D.C.: National Geographic Kids, 2016.

On the Web

With an adult, learn more online with these suggested searches.

National Fire Protection Association website

National Junior Firefighter Program website

Smokey for Kids website

Glossary

arson (AR-suhn) the crime of setting property on fire with the intention of destroying it

cardiopulmonary resuscitation (kahr-dee-oh-PUL-muh-nair-ee ri-suh-suh-TAY-shuhn) also called CPR; an emergency lifesaving procedure used when someone's heart stops beating

combustible (kuhm-BUH-stuh-buhl) able to catch fire and burn easily

hydraulic ladders (hye-DRAW-lik LAD-uhrz) ladders powered by moving liquid through pipes under pressure

jaws of life (JAWZ UHV LYFE) a heavy-duty tool used to cut through metal or pry it apart to rescue trapped people

oxidation (ahk-suh-DAY-shuhn) a chemical reaction that happens when a substance comes into contact with oxygen

stamina (STAM-uh-nuh) the physical and mental ability to do demanding tasks for a long period of time

stop, drop, and roll (STAHP, DRAHP, AND ROHL) a simple fire safety procedure used to smother flames when a person's clothes are on fire

toxic (TAHK-sik) poisonous or capable of causing injury or death

Index